WARREN PULLEY

Entrepreneur.com

10 Steps To Starting Your Business and Dominating Your Market

RYPUL MEDIA

First published by RyPul Media 2021

Copyright © 2021 by Warren Pulley

All rights reserved. No part of this publication may be reproduced, stored or transmitted in any form or by any means, electronic, mechanical, photocopying, recording, scanning, or otherwise without written permission from the publisher. It is illegal to copy this book, post it to a website, or distribute it by any other means without permission.

Warren Pulley asserts the moral right to be identified as the author of this work.

Warren Pulley has no responsibility for the persistence or accuracy of URLs for external or third-party Internet Websites referred to in this publication and does not guarantee that any content on such Websites is, or will remain, accurate or appropriate.

Designations used by companies to distinguish their products are often claimed as trademarks. All brand names and product names used in this book and on its cover are trade names, service marks, trademarks and registered trademarks of their respective owners. The publishers and the book are not associated with any product or vendor mentioned in this book. None of the companies referenced within the book have endorsed the book.

First edition

*This book was professionally typeset on Reedsy.
Find out more at reedsy.com*

To My Air Force Drill Sergeants Who Taught Me To...
"Aim High...Fly-Fight-Win,"

Contents

Preface		ii
1	Market Research Is King	1
2	Beast Your Business Plans	5
3	How To Fund Startup's Wisely	10
4	The Best Location Wins	15
5	Should I Choose An LLC or Corporation?	18
6	Business Branding Matters	22
7	Great Legal Represenation Matters	26
8	Federal and State Tax ID Numbers	30
9	Why Business Licenses and Permits	32
10	Business Banking Explained	36
11	101 Business Terms You Need To Know	40
12	You're An Entrepreneur	53
About the Author		55

Preface

Money creates the opportunity for a better quality of life choices and a more meaningful human existence when you can use your wealth for the betterment of humanity. For a business person, there is no doubt that the desire for financial freedom motivates many of their decision when starting new business ventures as well as their personal desire to improve the quality of life for themselves and their families.

The entrepreneurial spirit has driven some of the wealthiest people to build huge fortunes around the world, and it continues to motivate the average person to build their own fortunes and family legacies through business.

My own personal experience and research have shown me that one of the best ways to achieve financial freedom is to start your own business. And I like many others have found business success within the fields of security, consulting, media, and marketing. I have also found that being a jack of all trades can be a great business strategy when used properly. I do believe that one thing we can all agree on is that the internet has opened up the world for entrepreneurs to market themselves globally, thereby increasing sales and service provider opportunities, which in turn makes it more likely you will become a success if you learn, test and apply solid business side management principles to your venture.

As a reminder, the internet has many free tools and resources which allow people to advertise online, build websites, create blogs, write articles, etc. The internet is the greatest tool ever created to help you launch, maintain and scale your business, if nothing else you should spend some time on the internet so that you become intimately familiar with how to find and capture your customer base.

Trust me your customer base is on the internet and so should you.

In short, the biggest mistake many people make when planning to start a business is to believe that they must become an expert in every aspect of their business before they start. I find this to be the biggest hindrances of most people seeking to start a business, they spend quite a lot of time thinking "about how to do", instead of putting a solid business plan in place and attacking the market full force. Remember, there are a number of free tools and resources available for people to learn about different aspects of business, but before you start your business, you need to know everything you can about your business and the aspects of the business you want to become an expert in.

These two things are a must for all entrepreneurs.

One is to be a problem solver, as you need to be able and willing to solve problems, which are posed by others, in a way that is beneficial for you or your business. You do not need to be an expert at problem-solving, but you need to know what you need to do.

And two is to focus on your strengths and take action on them. Focus on your strengths and talents. Take advantage of opportunities to develop your strengths by learning from others who have overcome real or imagined challenges. In your business, you need to recognize and capitalize on your strengths in order to grow your business into whatever it is you want it to be.

If you want to build a business that is of benefit to you, your family, and your community, and you have the right attitude, you will be able to pull this off, tell yourself right now that there is no more time for talk, it's time to get to work.

1

Market Research Is King

This may very well be the most important step you take, which is likely to determine the success or failure of your business model. There are several ways you can use market research to your advantage, with most of the most effective ways is figuring out how to engage your potential consumer base in your research plans.

You can use market research to provide consumers with information about your business to help them make an informed decision. These surveys usually consist of multiple questions asked by a selection of respondents in an effort to determine their preferences and trends. Each individual survey question is often grouped with similar questions to yield a total response from the panel. Consumers may select one of five responses to a question, each response representing one percent of the total responses. Respondents will generally select one response from each group.

As you develop your business plan, incorporate market research into your analysis of your business prospects. Assess the potential impact of your business idea on a variety of consumer groups. Use this information to refine your market research, and to add detail to your business idea. As you develop your plan, include information about your potential markets and benefits. You can then add details such as your competitors, your market segmentation, your advantages, and your disadvantages.

This data will prove invaluable when you go before an investor to raise money for your business. You can use market research to analyze trends, such as the decline in home shopping, and the growth in big-box retail.

You can also use the information to improve your business idea. For example, you might discover that your customers are women, aged 25 to 34, who earn $40,000-$60,000 per year. If your business idea is to sell cosmetics, you might want to include the youth segment as a potential target market. By looking at the age of consumers, you might discover that women, in their early 20's, might not be interested in having a full line of makeup. But, they might also be interested individually in lip gloss, eye shadow, mascara, and other beauty products.

You can develop your plan and your business idea with this information. But, you can't develop your plan and your business idea without specific data on your competitors. In refining your market research you have to consider the number of competitors you have, their demographic and/or geographic distribution, their sales performance, their marketing strategies, their strengths and weaknesses, and any special features or advantages that they may have over you.

The best way to incorporate market research in your business plan is to incorporate it in your marketing plan. You can't get around the fact that you have to convince the buying public about your business before you can get them to invest in you. But, you can improve your chances of success by carefully analyzing what your competitors are doing to get the buying public to believe in you. This is true market research. And, although it's not as objective as competitive analysis, it is more complete than a "market-based" plan. But it's also more costly, time-consuming, and frustrating because, unlike competitive analysis, you can't learn what your competitors are doing simply by reading the business plans of your competitors. But this is essential if you are to beat them.

Here are the top 3 essential market research tips you should focus on.

1. The first thing to understand about market research is that it's not a competition. Competition is a situation in which one company tries to gain an advantage over another company by offering its products or services at a lower price or by offering products and/or services at a faster delivery time. Market research is a situation in which you try to gain an understanding of what consumers want, need, and want to buy. It's not a competition.

2. Market research is a situation where the goal is not only to gain an advantage over your competition but also to gain an advantage over your competitors among the different markets. It is not a situation where you are trying to reach a perfect solution among a myriad of imperfect products and services.

In other words, market research is not a situation in which you try to add more value to what you offer.

3. Market research is a situation where you try to add value (improve) to what you offer, rather than trying to take value away from what you offer. For example, if you are offering a movie ticket, you'd probably want to add value to your offer by adding extras, such as snacks, drinks, and drinks with a short presentation time. If you are offering a college course, you'd probably want to take value away from your offering by not including audio and video recordings.

~End of Chapter 1~

2

Beast Your Business Plans

A good business plan guides you through each stage of starting and managing your business. It outlines the key steps you'll need to accomplish in each stage and puts you in touch with your business's opportunities and threats so you can plan responses in advance.

A plan is an important part of your business planning for many reasons. It:

1. Shapes your thinking - it's an excellent way to get your thinking in order. It helps you to prioritize your goals.

2. Identifies your target market - your target market defines your market because it includes both the people who are already buying your products and the people who are going to be buying them in the future.

3. Shapes your marketing - marketing is very much about relating your business to your target market. A good marketing

plan will help you to connect the way you speak and the way your products look to the way your products are perceived by your target market.

4. Shapes your financial position - a plan can help you to decide how you'll fund your business. It will help you plan how much and what type of financial products you'll be taking on.

5. Shapes your management structure - a plan helps you to decide how you'll organize your management team. It will help you to decide who will manage your day-to-day operations.

A plan is about more than just writing down your goals and what you want to accomplish in each stage. It is also about deciding what you'll do in each stage. When you have written a plan you should also write your results and your experience in each stage so you can see how your plan fits your results. It is also a great way to move forward when you get stuck. You can always look at your plan to see where you are and where you are going.

A plan is your business' foundation. You should write a plan from the beginning to the end so you have a visual representation of your business. This way you can look at it regularly to see how you're doing and you'll know how to keep moving forward. Your plan should include each of the following:

1. Mission

2. Market

3. Mission of specific products

4. Goals

5. Results

6. Experience

7. Structure

8. Manage and Structure

9. Focus

10. Financial

11. Marketing

12. Sales

13. Product Development

14. Product Testing

Remember that each step should be carefully considered so that your business can be more effective. Make sure that you structure your plan in a way that will easily allow you to stay on track. If you find that you are going off track it is a good idea to look at your plan from different angles to see where you should go. It is also a good idea to revisit your plan a few times throughout the year to see how your progress is coming along.

You should now have a clear picture of what your business should look like and where it should be. Now it's time to put it all together. It is also a good idea to look at your plan from different perspectives to see how you can be more effective.

The final steps of a plan are to make sure that your business can be more effective. This means that you have to put everything together and make sure that it works together. For example, when considering a marketing strategy make sure that you are considering how you are going to communicate your messages to your customers.

Remember that in order to be more effective your plan should include every aspect of your business. When you are working on your plan you should know what needs to happen to make your business more effective. You should know what your customers need and want and you should know what your customers have come to expect. You should know what tools are available to you and you should know how you can motivate your employees. These are all part of your plan and you should know them very well. These are the elements that should be included in your plan so that when you start implementing your plan you will know exactly how everything works together.

For most small businesses, the plan is the most important document that they produce. This is due to the fact that it defines where your business is now and where it is going. It will give you an idea of how many customers you have and how many customers you need. It will also tell you how many employees you need and how much money you need to run your business. For most small businesses, this document is very important because it gives them a clear idea of how their business operates. It will give your manager an idea of how many sales he needs to achieve certain targets and it will help your accountant to know how much profits your business should earn to pay your employees.

Your plan should include every aspect of your business. It is important that the plan includes every aspect of your business because it is a document that you use every day. You should know that if your business is not effective then it could cause you problems. A plan is your business operating manual. For most small businesses the plan will be the one that they use to measure whether they are doing their job well.

For most small businesses the plan is the most important document that they produce. This is due to the fact that it defines where your business is now and where it is going.

It will give you an idea of how many customers you have and how many customers. It will also tell you how many employees you need and how much money you need to run your business. For most small businesses, this document is very important because it gives them a clear idea of how their business operates.

~End of Chapter 2~

3

How To Fund Startup's Wisely

Any entrepreneur will tell you that the hardest thing to do is raise money to start your own business. Many potential entrepreneurs are discouraged because they believe that there is no way to get enough money to start their own business.

Without a solid track record, it may be impossible to obtain a bank loan or to obtain financing from a venture capitalist. If financing options such as credit and lines of credit are out of reach, under certain circumstances you can turn to social media platforms that have donated money to help small businesses succeed. Crowdfunding sites such as Kickstarter, Indiegogo, and GoFundMe, are great sources of funding with the right business proposition pitch. You can also set up a 30-day fundraiser to attract donations from the Kiva credit community, or invite friends and family to help you with financing.

For those of you not familiar with the crowdfunding model, it's easily explained as a practice of raising money from a large group of people, for a specific purpose, normally in small donation amounts with the goal of raising large sums of capital from people who believe in your idea or product and would like to become a part of creating something from scratch, when used properly it can be a viable way of financing small entrepreneurs. This form of financing is definitely the most common way for companies to raise money for their start-ups.

You don't necessarily need to be tech-savvy to launch a crowdfunding campaign, but you do need to focus all your energy on making your business profitable. If you want to raise money for your start-up company. As we discussed earlier this is when one of your companies most important documents will come into play and that's your business plan because investors will want to see it.

Angel investors who put money into startups will want to hear and see the business ideas that will provide them a return on investment (ROI) that they can live with. Your business plan should be as detailed as possible and provide answers to all the sticking points investors look at before they are willing to invest their own money. What you need is a strong marketing plan that puts your launches in context - the growth potential of your brand, product, or idea and either you or your brand representative should possess the ability to interact with a cash-rich community, and be as persuasive as possible.

Selling your business idea and raising capital revolves around setting the perfect tone for your business and what you can do for investors who you can encourage them to fund it. Even if it may be only an idea at this stage, crowdfunding is a great example of how you can raise money for a product.

Another great source for connecting with venture capitalists is by way of promoting your business venture on social media platforms. One very useful way of doing so is by engaging with your local Small Business Administration or SBA's investment fund to find potential investors, this is a great resource many startups often overlook, and while the SBA may seem like another impenetrable government-funded entity with an endless phone tree you would need to access in order to speak with a live person, I have found in my dealing with the SBA, that your local SBA counselor or representative is very responsive, helpful and provides very informative ways for you to reach the success you seek, in the areas of business planning, funding, and the accessing of local business services.

Please understand that this is not an endorsement for the SBA, however, it is a valuable resource that should not be overlooked.

For those operating on a tight budget and looking for more capital, another great resource is the traditional route of applying for a small business loan with a local bank or major bank if your long-term goal is to grow your brand outside of your local marketplace.

Another term that you should become intimately familiar with is *"seed financing"* which helps you raise money for market research, hiring a team, and developing your product or service, while venture capitalists help you expand your reach.

If your start-up does not require large initial costs, other options include providing bootstrapping, asking family and friends for help, or taking out a small business loan. Avoid the traditional route of bank loans, but there are many options for small loans – business loans and start-up financing. This may seem like an impossible feat, and with a bit of luck and a bit of hard work, it can be. If you have ever tried to build your own business then you know that finding the money to get started can be one of the biggest obstacles you face. One of the many things you have to consider when funding your business is explained in depth over the next few paragraphs.

In the beginning stages of funding round(s), you should ensure that you have direct access to sound financial business planners who can help you understand the ramifications of selling a portion of your company for funds, taking on debt to secure funding, borrowing money from banks or crowdfunding from social media or friends and family. It's always a good business practice to seek out experts who can explain the benefits of raising capital to start, grow of continually fund your business pursuits.

The entrepreneur's contribution to the company will only be as strong as the entrepreneur's understanding of the equity, ROI, business strategy, growth strategy, inbound and outbound market, and the value of your product or service. This understanding will only be as strong as the entrepreneur's willingness to listen to their employees, their board, legal counsel, or CFO and make sure they understand that their contribution is important and that they are making an informed decision.

If you come into the process thinking your the smartest person in the room and that you can go it alone without oft-needed expertise, you can be certain to you are ringing the death knell for your company long term. Wise up early by placing the proper people in places to help you become successful, you won't regret it.

~End of Chapter 3~

4

The Best Location Wins

When it comes to starting a small business or any business for that matter, the location itself is a major part of the recipe for its success. Research by many of the worlds leading business associations has shown that the location you choose for your business is by far the most important factor in business success. The location determines factors such as start-up costs, supply chain support, the demographic makeup of your customers, qualified workforce sourcing, access to shipping, transportation or storage hubs if required, the local business climate, and infrastructure concerns such as internet services, affordable office space and product demand for your service, product or brand.

The mentality of your customers and the aura of a particular region are also factors that must be taken into account when choosing a location for your small business. For example, if your business is based on selling school supplies, demographic research on the right location should keep in mind that it is located near schools near universities and colleges in your area.

The key is to consider the main problems that companies face when choosing a location and to consider the most appropriate way to make a choice. The following factors should help you choose the location for your small business. Check local and state laws that affect running a business from home, as zoning laws can sometimes be an important factor in deciding what type of business you want to start.

To do this, you might want to consider what small business owners are generally looking for in business facilities and how these facilities can support their business. Before you choose your first business facility, you should take some time to find out which facilities you need. If you are starting a business, you should not start without important business elements, as you do not want to be distracted and lose elements that are not important for small businesses, such as an office, warehouse, or parking lot.

Your local Small Business Administration has a list outlining the joint federal business licenses that are required based on your industry, which is a good starting point for research. If you want to grow your business, it can be beneficial to work with a small business specialist or consultant in your local community. Other location-specific business consulting can help you choose a company name, create a logo and register the company, to comply with local ordinances and laws.

Although the perfect location is different for each business, covering these critical areas offers the best chance to thwart failure scenarios and stay on track towards your future success. Remember that the right business locations are important to provide business facilities and that you need to spend as much time as possible finding the "perfect" location.

You can significantly increase the chances of acquiring business facilities that make a positive contribution to your profits by carefully weighing up what functions these facilities need to perform for your businesses. If you're thinking about a particular location that would give your start-up an added edge over the competition, read our guide to the best business start-up locations in the United States.

~End of Chapter 4~

5

Should I Choose An LLC or Corporation?

Choosing a corporate structure for your business is one of the most important steps in establishing your business.

Whether you want to buy an existing business or start a new one, you need to decide which type of business (also known as a "business structure" or business unit) is best for you. An important step is to decide how the business should be structured and whether you want to change the corporate structure for legal or financial reasons. There are many different business structures available to new independent entrepreneurs who are just starting up a business.

The type of business structure you choose determines the form for your income tax return and can affect how you structure your health care benefits for your family and employees. Your tax advisor will advise you on the various types of corporate structures, including sole proprietorship's, partnerships, joint ventures, limited liability companies, and corporations.

SHOULD I CHOOSE AN LLC OR CORPORATION?

Corporate structures such as sole proprietorship's - business owners and partnerships do not require personal taxes because they have something called a passport - through taxation. Companies pay income tax on profits, although there are some rules that your lawyer can explain to you if you are interested in this or any other type of corporate structure.

If any of these options feel right for you, you should consult a legal or financial professional to help you determine which business structure works best for your business. If you are not sure what type of corporate structure is right for you and your business, you can consult legal and financial experts to determine whether this type of company is right.

Before you put together your business plan, it is crucial to decide what kind of legal business structure you will have. I would also recommend that you consult a business lawyer before setting up a business organization until you are certain that the structure you have decided on is the best financial and business operations best for your specific business needs.

As you can see, there are many types of companies, each of which has a different legal structure. Most entrepreneurs will, however, choose one of the three legal corporate structures, such as a public limited company, a joint venture, or a non-profit organization.

A sole proprietorship is the simplest and most common structure to choose for starting a business. It is essentially a situation where someone is doing business and no other type of business is registered, so there is no difference between business owners.

A sole proprietorship is a common choice for adding partners or employees and it is one of the simplest business structures under which a profit-based company can operate.

Every business situation is different, but there are clear advantages to starting an LLC. If you still have doubts (I would suggest consulting a business lawyer), you can consider choosing either an LLC (Limited Liability Company) or an S Company if there is any doubt.

If you live in a City or State where litigation is common, an LLC as a business structure can protect your personal assets. If your industry is vulnerable to lawsuits, you can opt for a corporate structure such as an LLP (company) where your liabilities are limited and do not extend to your personal assets. You can protect yourself and your company from the actions of your employees through the official business structures that are intended for LLCs and companies. If you find that your business is low risk and you do not want the administrative burden of a company or LLC, you can choose a sole proprietorship or partnership. A sole proprietorship is best suited to start-up owners who want to retain control of their business and have the negotiating ability to develop partnership contracts.

If you want to start your business with one or more partners, a business partnership is a simple business structure that can take this into account. If you start the business without a partner, you would have to choose a partnership with higher corporate structures.

When you have reached this phase of starting your business, I highly recommend that you seek professional legal advice on how to form your company and which structure works best for your specific situation.

~End of Chapter 5~

6

Business Branding Matters

So now it's time we discuss how to name your company and how important it is to choose an effective company name. A few things to consider are to find out what you can use in your company name, and what you should do before you choose a creative company name.

One of the first things you would need to do is to secure a domain name that matches the company name which you have decided on, a good rule of thumb is to make a list of possible names and go through them one by one to see which domain names you could also buy. For social media wide brand representation and recognition it's important that your company name, website address, logo, social media accounts, and business-related documents all speak the same language, e.g. email accounts, logo colors, fonts, messages, and customer-facing images which support your brand messaging. If you like one of the domain names on the list and you think it is suitable for your business, you can choose one of them.

You probably won't be able to choose a name that conveys everything you want to carry with your brand, so prioritize your list and see how many items you can tick off the different names you can imagine. When you think through your company's name, check that it matches your company's brand name and the no other names on the list of currently incorporated companies.

When creating your website, your domain name should be closely linked to the name of your company. If you plan to have a website that your customers can visit, you should first look for available domain names before committing to a name for your business. Whether you like every name on the market or not, there is should be solid research on your part to determine which name your competitors have chosen and to select a name that stands out from your competition and allows you to be unique, memorable, and competitive.

Choose a company name that connects you to your brand, and of course, make sure that the name is available to you. If you are just starting out, you want to choose a name that will become a banner for your company. For example, if you start a blog, or even just for a website or social media site, you want to be able to find the right name for it that matches the brand name of your website, blog, or other website content. Choose names that make it painfully obvious what your company, brand, or service is for so that potential customers don't have to guess what you're selling.

If you want your name to stand out and still be memorable, make sure it sounds good out loud. If you are looking for a way to choose a business name, using a personal name or nickname may work just as well, if not better, than a brand name. Whichever method you use to choose to name your company name, you will come up with something great, with a little bit of creativity.

If you find a name that meets the above criteria, you must register your company name as a business entity. Before choosing the best brand name for your business, you should consider the corporate structure you want to include in your brand names.

If you follow these tips on naming your company, you can choose the best brand name for your business. There are good free tools online to help you in brainstorming a domain name or business name. You can also create long lists of company names and ideas by using the word dump from the company name generators free online.

A strong business name is the foundation of your business success, and you can make the most of your company name by creating a name that will serve you well. Once you know how to choose a company with a unique and recognizable name, you are well on the way to marketing success when you start your business.

Creative company names provide tons of potential branding options, as a reminder thinks through your business model, your service, or product niche then choose wisely.

Don't overthink this, as it's important to get the business of business.

~End of Chapter 6~

7

Great Legal Represenation Matters

Before you start a business, it is important not to forget to go through the formal process of registering your business. In most states, including California, fictitious company names can be registered with the Secretary of State or other state agencies, but in some states, they are registered with a separate organization such as an LLC or corporation. Registering a company name is usually as easy as registering with a state or federal agency, such as the Your jurisdictions Secretary of State, the Securities, and Exchange Commission, or the Federal Trade Commission.

Get a state tax identification and permit: Once you know the state or states where you will operate your business, check with each jurisdiction to determine what licenses and permits may be required for your business to operate. If you find that you need a sales tax permit to sell retail, you should contact states and local governments to understand your obligations regarding property, income, and employment taxes.

Depending on the structure and location of your company,

you can register with your state or federal government or not, depending on the structure, location, and business.

If you run a professional business, you need a business license from the state or federal government, as well as a license or permit. The procedure for submitting a business license varies from license to license, but you can generally find out about obtaining your business license on the websites of districts, states, and states.

This means that almost every type of company should be registered with an official authority at the local, state, or federal level. In addition to registering your company name with the state, you must register the company in the city or county where you operate it. If you register your name in a city, district, city, district, district, or district office, you will also need a trade registration card or other proof that you registered it in that city or district.

If your business needs to be licensed in the state of Colorado, you must register with the regulatory authority. If you are a resident of Illinois and intend to do business within Illinois as a legal entity, you must register with the Illinois Secretary of State. Ultimately, the licensing and permitting requirements for businesses depend on your city or county. Therefore, always check with your state and local jurisdiction to ensure that you have the licenses and permits necessary to operate your business the way you do, to avoid fees and legal complications. This varies from city to city and state to state, but always check the policies of local governments when you start a business.

When you register your company with your state, you will receive a government identification number that allows you to pay state taxes on behalf of your employees. The EIN, also known as Federal Tax ID, is a 9-digit number issued by the IRS to identify you as a business and is also known as an employer identification number (A).

The EIN identifies you as a company for tax purposes and is used in the same way as your driving license, social security number, and other government identification numbers. You can use it to open commercial bank accounts, apply for business licenses or register your business with the IRS.

If you apply for registration of your company name as a federal or state trademark, you must apply separately for registration of a company - the application for registration of a name. You will file an application with the United States Patent and Trademark Office to make it a registered trademark for the federal government. If you are not required to do so, you should register as an LLC in your state.

Your registrar must be resident in the state where you wish to register your business and obtain all legal and official documents on behalf of your business. Make sure that all contacts you have selected for the company have access to all the necessary documents that you will receive from the authorities under which the company is to be registered.

If you are thinking about starting a business but are not yet sure what legal forms you need, it's important for you to seek legal counsel to assist you in properly registering your company to conduct business ethically and legally.

~End of Chapter 7~

8

Federal and State Tax ID Numbers

For many of us, the Internal Revenue Service (IRS) requires us to submit an employer identification number (EIN), also called a tax identification number it is required for most companies. The EIN is assigned by the IRS for business registration and reporting purposes and must have a number of digits (you can imagine it as your company's Social Security number).

It also acts as an employer identification number, which is used when paying taxes to the federal government. It is also known as the Federal Tax Identification Number (also known as EIN or FEIN) or sometimes as the Social Security Number or Federal Employee Identification Number (FEDIN). It is commonly used in connection with accounting and taxes, and for other business purposes.

The Employer Identification Number (EIN) gives your company an identification number and is, at least for the IRS, the most important part of your federal tax identification number. It is your Social Security Number (SSN) for business and it is a unique number assigned to the business so that the Internal Revenue Service (IRS) and the U.S. Department of Health and Human Services (HHS) can easily identify it as a business.

This is the number the IRS uses to identify your business and must be included in all of the company's federal tax filings. The employer ID number is used by the IRS to identify you as a company. This number and any other information about your employer and the tax status of your company, such as the company name and address of your employees, must be included in your company's tax filings.

If you are a sole proprietor, using an EIN means you do not need to provide a Social Security number on your W-9 form. If you have employees, you do not necessarily need to use a Social Security number (SSN) as your tax identification number, as the one is designed for corporate-to-corporate tax returns. The IRS issues an employer identification number that small businesses can use to identify themselves.

This unique nine-digit number that the IRS issues to companies for tax identification purposes is one of the most common tax identification numbers in the US and the only one available to companies with employees or employees of employees. It is a nine-digit number assigned to a company for identification by the IRS and subject to the same rules of procedure as the Social Security number.

~End of Chapter 8~

9

Why Business Licenses and Permits

A business license is a government-issued permit that gives you permission to operate your business in your specified jurisdiction, operating documents can allow you to operate regionally, nationally, or internationally.

In this chapter, we will explain the different types of licenses and permits for businesses, including the ones you need to start a business. If you need one and how to get it, do you know what it is and what it is for? The most basic type of business license you might need is your local operating license, which essentially grants you the right to operate your businesses, as the name suggests.

Not all licenses and permits are required for each company, and you will need to do further research that will apply to your particular company. In addition to a business license, you also need a business license to regulate the permits of your company, to name just a few. To find out exactly what licenses or permits your companies need, check out the small business websites linked to each state or country in which you live, You will find that they will determine the licensing and approval requirements of your state or location and provide you with information on how to obtain a business license. Use this information to create a list of the general licenses and permits required, and then add the licenses that most companies require. What kind of license or permit your business needs depends on where you live and in which industries you are active.

While most companies require a standard business license, you may also need special licenses or permits for certain industries, please ensure you ask the right questions from your local permitting officials, or employ a business lawyer to help you sort things out.

In some states, you must have several different types of licenses or permits, which have different requirements depending on the type of business you are setting up, the employees you have, and the products or services you sell. What kind of license you need depends on the type of business you are doing and where you are doing business, again make certain that you have obtained all of the necessary permits before you begin business operations, not doing so could end your endeavor in very short order.

There are a number of different types of licenses and authorizations, some of which may apply to e-commerce companies and some to retail businesses, ensure you know which type to seek, apply for and obtain.

Environmental and small business licenses and permits are mostly state and federal, but it is worth noting because they also list local permitting requirements.

Once you have obtained the appropriate business permits, you may need to show your trade license at the company's headquarters. Determine whether your license as an LLC or Corporation is required to be posted as well.

If your business is involved in an activity that is supervised or regulated by a federal agency, you may need to obtain federal licenses and permits. Federal licenses or permits are required if your companies engage in activities that are regulated or supervised by federal agencies. If your business license or permit is required for a company involved in activities regulated by any of these federal departments or agencies, such as the Food and Drug Administration (FDA), the Environmental Protection Agency (EPA), or the Department of Justice (DOJ), ensure that you have met all Federal permitting requirements before you begin business operations.

If your business is involved in an activity that is supervised or regulated by any of these federal agencies, you may need to obtain a special license, certification, or permit in addition to any other required licenses or permits. The procedure for applying for a business license varies from license to license, but information about acquiring business licenses is generally available on the websites of districts, states, and states. Just make sure that submitting all the licenses and permits you need is at the top of your list.

Note

WHY BUSINESS LICENSES AND PERMITS

The process for obtaining a business license depends on the license you need and the state or country in which you operate, and we always recommend you seek legal advice to help you apply for a license and ensure compliance.

If you are thinking of starting your own business, it is important to read our guide to the required registration and registration requirements for businesses in your state or county.

You can work with your local government to find out what licenses you need to start your business. Before going through the different types of business licenses, you can discuss which ones you will need. Don't forget to consult with the SBA or local authorities or authorities about assistance in obtaining the licenses necessary for the establishment of your business.

We wish you the best of luck on your journey!

~End of Chapter 9~

10

Business Banking Explained

One of the most important aspects of protecting your business interest is to ensure that you keep your business and personal banking separate and exclusive, as commingling personal and business account monies can lead to severe financial penalties as well as loss of certain legal protections afforded to your business in the way of certain civic liability issues.

Opening a business bank account is one way to separate your business and personal spending. It can be used to check the legitimacy of the company when it is time to apply for credit cards and corporate loans. A bank account for a company is a professional means of doing business and allows you to be professional. Opening a business bank account can show the world that you are able to manage business finances with business accounts and checks to pay for supplies and services.

The type of documents required to open a commercial bank account depends on the type of company and bank. If you are starting your business or moving it to a new institution, you will need to present several documents such as your incorporation documents, personal identification, business license, operating permits, and EIN issued by the US Government. if you are incorporating and operating your business within the United States. If you plan to open a business bank account, you may want to collect this information in advance.

Firstly, business owners must provide more information before signing up for a business bank account. If you plan to open a business bank account, whether in person or online, you will also need the name, address, phone number, and email address of the business owner, as well as a copy of the company license and business card number.

Opening a commercial bank account is similar, except that you must provide business information. LLC, you must apply for a Business Bank account and open it with your name, address, phone number, and business card number, as well as a copy of your company license.

A commercial bank account allows you to separate your personal finances from your business finances, as you are legally required to do so if you operate the business as a legal entity, such as an LLC or corporation. To improve the records, it helps you to have a separate business and bank account, prove that you are a legitimate business and not a hobby. You can only open a company account if your company is an LLP, LLC, corporation, or sole proprietorship.

If you want your customers to be able to write checks in your company name, you need a corporate bank account. If you can accept checks that were issued in the company's name, then you are likely to have an account with a local bank, such as Bank of America, Wells Fargo, or the Federal Reserve.

You should open your bank account as soon as you start accepting and spending money as a business, but if you don't have one yet, you need to open it as your business grows. If you are legally required to open it, an employer ID number (EIN) ensures that you are kept informed of any expenses and payments received. One of the most important aspects of opening a bank account for companies that we need to take into account is what charges are levied.

Whether you are starting an LLC, corporation, or partnership, keeping a business bank account can help you avoid unnecessary problems.

Opening a business bank account can also help you save time by streamlining your company's financial records and tax information. Given the other benefits of a Business Bank account, we recommend that you obtain a separate Business Account for companies that fall under the jurisdiction of the Internal Revenue Service (IRS). It makes it easier for you to manage your finances and support the company, and it is also more efficient.

Each bank has different requirements, so you should check with your bank before trying to open a commercial bank account. Make sure that the bank you are opening your commercial bank account with has all the tools you need to manage your money. Ask them before you make any decisions about whether or not you want to open a business bank account for your company or a separate business account.

Read on and you will learn more about how to open a bank account and how this can benefit your business. Learn how commercial bank accounts can work and make a banking decision that is best for you and your business. Find out why you should have a Business Bank account and what you need to do before you open an account.

As a reminder, The Internal Revenue Service (IRS) can check your personal bank details to find business transactions and decides to audit your business. It is essential that you determine whether you normally need a special bank account for the company, and if not, you have the option of not having a separate business bank account. T

To avoid confusion and potential problems with IRS, it is absolutely essential that you keep all your business and personal financial information separate without fail.

Lastly, setting up an accounting system for your businesses is also a very important legal step that cannot be understated, and determines whether or not you need an account with a local bank or a national bank such as Bank of America or HSBC. It is very important that you keep copious, strict financial records of your business operations as a matter of best business practices. These records can be helpful to your company for credit, legal and operation reasons.

~End of Chapter 10~

11

101 Business Terms You Need To Know

The first thing you need to know is that there are hard and fast rules when it comes to the language of business, it is imperative to the success of your business that you speak the common language of established business moguls as well as the language of the startup. Once you understand and commit the following terms and phrases to memory, there is a whole world of possibilities that you can explore and a considerations you can exploit in order to grow your business successfully and establish yourself as a smart, effective business person among your peer group, to your customer, clients, vendors and employees.

In other words DON'T BE A DUMMY its imperative that you learn the language of your chosen profession to ensure that your competence cannot be called into question.

These popular terms are ones that you are most likely to encounter on a daily basis, so be certain to read, research and understand each of these terms explicitly as the health of your company and its financial bottom line will most certainly depend on it.

Although these business terms are not listed in alphabetical order, the order in which they are listed do not denote one words as more important than another. Each of these terms carry the same weight in the daily operations and management of your business. So grab a cup of coffee and dig in.

Business Terms Listed and Defined:

Business plan: a written document of financial, operational, production and administrative tasks required for future business operations.

Monetization: the conversion of or implementation of revenue generating mechanisms into websites, usually through advertising.

Cash flow statement: a financial statement that shows how changes in balance sheet accounts and income affect the cash and cash equivalents of a company.

Margin: in commerce, the difference between the price of selling something and the cost of producing it. In equities trading, margin refers to the amount of money loan by a brokerage to a trader to place on trades beyond his regular balance.

Acquisition: the purchasing of an asset or firm by a party or company.

Competitor: a rival business interest which competes for the same market as another business.

Equity: ownership of an asset, above and beyond debt considerations.

Account: a record of the money a company pays out.

Revenue: the amount of money that a company receives in a given period.

Company: a commercial business.

Overhead: an integral cost to the production of goods or services.

Startup: a newly formed company that, usually through technological innovation, seeks to disrupt an industry.

Supply chain: a network of interlinked entities or businesses that contribute to delivering a product to the end user.

Disruption: an innovation of technology or practice that transforms the way business, manufacturing or other traditional processes occur by displacing other methods.

Accounting: process of financial record keeping, interpreting and communicating in business.

Lien: a creditor's conditional right of ownership against a debtor's asset or property that bars its sale or transfer without paying off the creditor.

Loan: an agreement for the temporary transfer of capital between one or more parties and other(s), usually with interest.

Agreement: an arrangement between two or more people, a contract.

Logistics: management of inventory that is in motion or at rest.

Contract: a legally binding agreement between parties, either written, spoken or implied.

Business: an organization, economic system or commercial activity in which goods or services are exchanged for money.

Downsizing: intentional reduction in workforce size to cut costs, become competitive or prepare for a buyout.

Budget: the amount of capital a business or organization has at its disposal for a specific or general purpose for a usually specific amount of time.

Personnel: the people or staff that are employed by a firm.

Sales department: department in a company responsible for finding new customers and making sales.

Presentation: a usually formal prepared demonstration of data, analysis, protocol or information delivered to a group of people.

Entrepreneur: an individual business founder and owner who often funds, develops and produces a product or service themselves.

Opportunity cost: a benefit, value or profit that must be given up in order to attain or pursue another opportunity.

Inventory: the assets, materials or products that a company owns or holds with the intentions of selling.

Party: entity or person that takes part or is involved in an agreement, lawsuit or transaction.

Liability: in finance, a claim against a company's assets. In accounting, liabilities are what a company owes to its creditors and employees.

Asset: an item which holds value or produces income.

Quarter: one of four three month intervals that comprise a company's fiscal year.

R&D: research and development – activity aimed at discovering solutions to problems or producing innovation or new products.

Investment: money committed or property acquired for future income.

VC: venture capital. Startup or growth equity capital or loan capital provided by private investors or specialized financial institutions.

Terms: conditions or stipulations that regulate or determine the nature of a contract, agreement or transaction.

Shareholder: an individual, group or organization that has an equity stake in a company.

Credit: in banking, credit refers to the ability of banks to create purchasing power from leveraging fractional reserves.

Capital: wealth in the form of money or assets, or money invested in a business to generate income.

Branding: the process involved in creating a unique name and image for a product in the mind of the consumer, chiefly through advertising campaigns.

Wholesale: bulk sales, rather than smaller individual retail sales.

Operations: jobs or tasks with one or more sub-tasks that transform data or resources into desired good, services or results.

CEO: the chief executive officer, or head of a company.

Income statement: a financial statement that measures a company's performance over a specific accounting period.

Project: a planned set of interrelated tasks that to be executed within a specific time frame.

Resign: to quit a job or position; to voluntarily leave employment with a firm.

CV: curriculum vitae. Also known as a resume, the CV is a summary of a job applicant's professional experience, educational background, references and other relevant information.

Transaction: usually a commercial exchange involving the swapping of good or services for capital.

Strategy: a method or plan designed to bring about a specific outcome.

Trademark: a specific symbol, logo or design used by firms for branding and identification purposes.

Deadline: the final time that a certain task must be completed by.

Conference call: also known as an analyst call, the conference call is a teleconferenced or live hosted event featuring presentations by the management and executives of a company and the company's investors and analysts.

Platform: a place or means for expression or operation; a framework for the operation of computer software.

Balance sheet: a summary of the financial balances of a corporation or business organization.

Status report: a business report that summarizes a particular situation as of a certain time and place.

Agenda: an ordered sequence of items discussed in a formal

meeting.

Partnership: a business organization in which two or more people pool their money, work and resources and share collectively in the profits and losses.

Merger: the voluntary amalgamation of two companies into a new, singular legal entity.

Social media: new media, especially mobile media, which relies on consumer interaction and content sharing.

Reach a consensus: achieve a unanimously agreed upon decision either within a group or between parties.

Exchange rate: the price at which the currency of one country can be traded for the currency of another countries.

Salary: a usually fixed amount of money paid by a company to an employee in exchange for their services.

Cost of sales: the total sum of all expenses required to produce a product for sale, including labor, rent, materials, equipment, etc.

Sponsor: firm that provides financial assistance to a company in exchange for advertising and promotional rights or space.

Launch: the process of introducing a new product or service into the marketplace.

Industry: economic activity concerned with the processing of raw materials and factory manufacturing, or a particular branch of specific economic activity.

Stakeholder: an individual, group, or organization that has an interest or concern in an organization.

Objective: a specific result or intended goal.

End user: the person or entity which actually uses a product or service.

Bonus: additional pay after salary given for performance reward or incentive.

Promotion: a position advancement within a company.

Market: a place where the forces of supply and demand operate and buyers and sellers interact to trade goods, capital or services.

Manager: the head of a specific company department, an executive officer.

Point of sale: the actual place where a product or service is sold to the end user.

Multitask: to do numerous, often unrelated jobs simultaneously.

CBA: cost benefit analysis. A process in which all costs associated with a specific project or endeavor are calculated and analyzed.

Networking: creating, maintaining and using connections with acquaintances and associates to both share and receive help with business, partnership or job opportunities.

Board of directors: the governing body of a firm, elected by the shareholders of the company to represent their interests.

Meeting: formal or informal gatherings of people or business people with a collective purpose.

Headquarters: a company's main office or administrative center. Example: The meeting today will be held at company headquarters.

Outsourcing: the contracting out of tasks by a company to usually lower cost regions or firms.

Profit: the total surplus remaining after all costs have been deducted.

Marketing: the process of choosing, developing and producing a product, its price, market, distribution channel and promotion to the consumer.

Staff: the entire group of employees who work at a company, or a specific group of employees working under a supervisor.

Consumer: an end user or purchaser of goods along the supply chain.

Viral marketing: explosive, rapid growth of a market or product/service sales, usually achieved through word of mouth advertising.

IT: information technology. A set of tools, processes, methodologies, data communications and the like employed to collect, process and present information.

Management: the organization and coordination of a business in order to achieve set objectives.

Telecommuting: Attending to one's work duties at home via virtual telecommunication instead of in-person office work. All virtual assistants telecommute to work.

Commercial: a paid advertisement on radio, television, or the internet.

Recruitment: the process of finding and hiring the best quality candidate for a position, either from outside a company or within.

Grant: a usually conditional gift or endowment of money by a company or organization for a specific use.

Bandwidth: another tech term that has made its way into the corporate environment. In day-to-day context, it is often used to ask if someone has time available to talk or work on a project.

Customer service department: the segment of a company that handles interactions between customers and the firm.

Scalable: a quality of certain systems that enable them to rapidly expand or contract business operations to meet the demands of a market.

Deliverable: this is a quantifiable good or service provided as a result of completing a project. A favorite term of project managers, this word has spread like a virus.

HR: human resources – the department which oversees hiring and manages the employees of a company.

Core Competency: when someone is competent, it hardly means that person is outstanding. But in business, core competencies refer to the things a company or a person does best.

Skill set: this refers to someone's range of skills. It's jargon because it's an unnecessary way of describing what could easily be referred to simply as "skills".

Price point: for some reason, some business types like to talk about "price points" instead of just "prices". This is one of many examples of using more complicated language in lieu of a simpler word or phrase.

Whether you're pitching your product or networking with others in your field, you may be seen as a more reputable colleague if you use the right terminology when you're talking. The fact is that corporate buzzwords will probably never go away, so it's important to learn to speak the lingo.

ENTREPRENEUR.COM

~End of Chapter 11~

12

You're An Entrepreneur

Congratulations!

You have now taken some of the most important steps to secure your future, becoming your own boss, and making your business a great success.

Now the hard work begins! From this point forward it's very important that you eat, sleep, and breathe your business, this is your new baby, and there is no amount of time, energy, support, or help that won't give to your new endeavor.

The success or failure of your new company completely depends on your dedication to its operation and health. Remember running a business is a long game, it's important that you not give up if you are not an instant hit, most companies take years to catch on and break even, but trust me, if you stick to the grind, you will be successful.

Everyone measures success differently, know what you consider success going into this process, and by all means and measures you should not consider success based on what you see other companies in your market doing, instead focus on your business model, growing market share, and set the standard for your business niche.

At the end of the day, you want the market following your lead!

Again, Congratulations, you are now an ENTREPRENEUR!

~End of Chapter 12~

About the Author

Warren is an entrepreneur who began his foray into business after working in several private industries and government positions. Warren is a business owner, military veteran, former police officer, private security contractor, and business consultant who thrives in helping startup companies move from concept to success.

Having gained his business experience while working his way up from several entry-level positions to the role of Chief Executive Officer for a major distribution company in California, Warren understands what it takes to make businesses successful, and he continues to share his knowledge through public speaking, writing books, podcasting, and business consulting.

Warren provides free business coaching to military veterans and shares his military, private protection, government consulting, and law enforcement experience in books and public speaking engagements.

You can connect with me on:
- https://www.rypulassessments.com
- https://twitter.com/RyContact
- https://www.facebook.com/RyPulMedia

www.ingramcontent.com/pod-product-compliance
Lightning Source LLC
Chambersburg PA
CBHW070317220526
45465CB00004B/1888